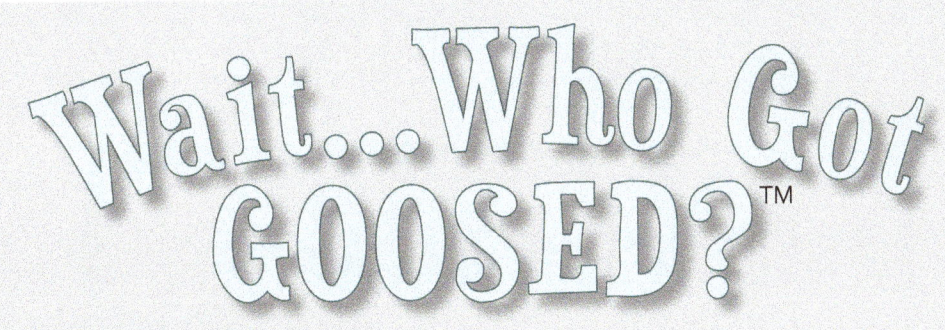

Wait...Who Got GOOSED?™

A COMPANION
Activity Book

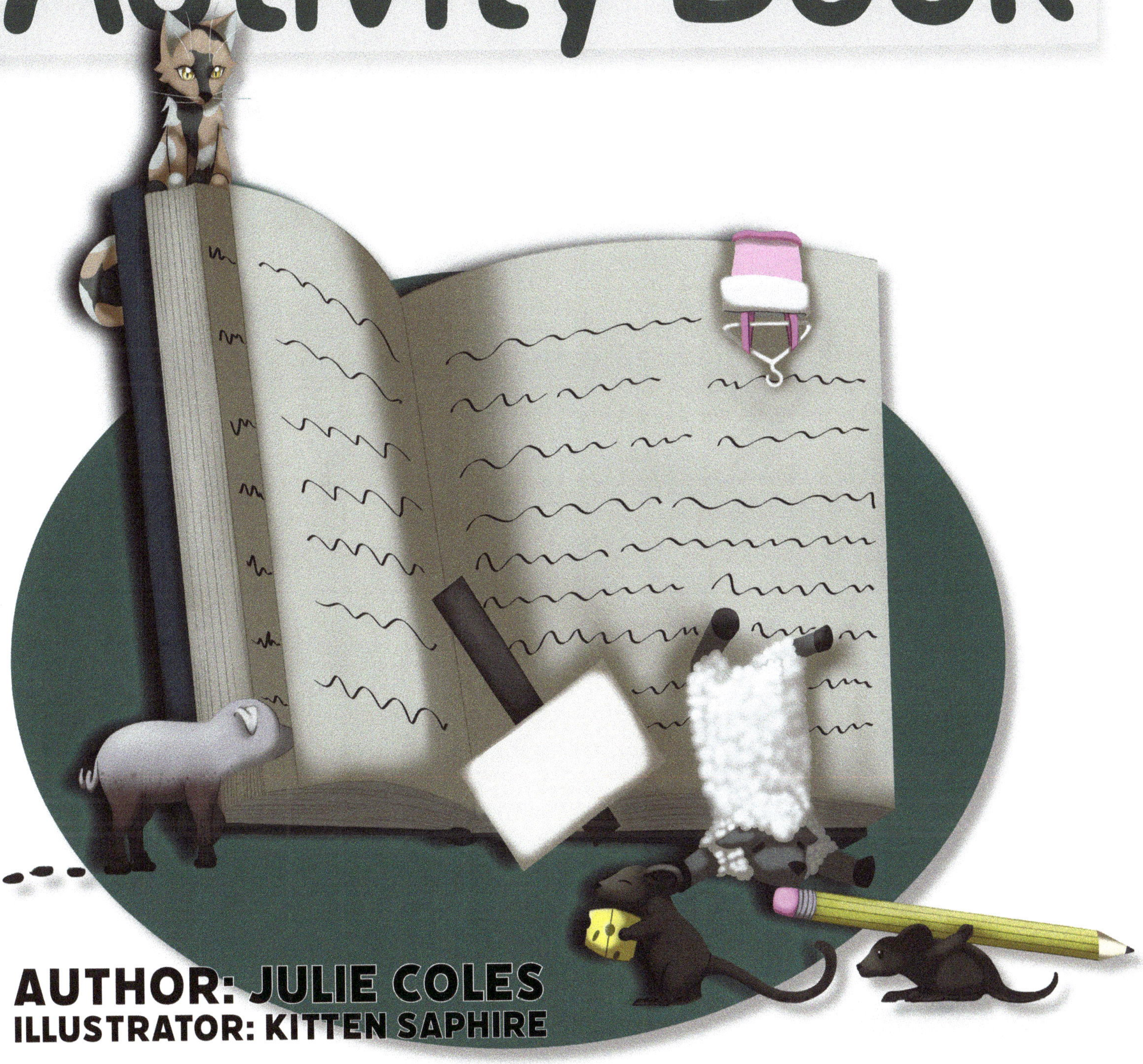

AUTHOR: JULIE COLES
ILLUSTRATOR: KITTEN SAPHIRE

This book belongs to:

_____

Wait…Who Got Goosed?™ A Companion Activity Book
Julie Coles
Published by Pivot In New Directions Publishing
Copyright © 2024 Julie Coles

ISBN (paperback):   978-1-954912-12-0
ISBN (e-Book):   978-1-954912-17-5

Copyeditor: Lisa Shrewsberry
Proofreader: Madison McMillion
Book Designer: Whitney Marshall, WMarshall Designs
Print Production: Michelle M. White, MMW Books
Illustrator: Kitten Saphire
Cover Designers: Kitten Saphire and Whitney Marshall, WMarshall Designs
Math Content Writer: Talya Marshall

Contact the author at
ImagineAMorePromisingFuture.com

Table of Contents

Welcome to Wait...Who Got Goosed?™
A Companion Activity Book

Tips for Using This Book

Resources you may find helpful...

- Wizard's Thinking Cap (Grab your favorite hat!)

- Human Resources (family member, friend, teacher)

- Other Valuable Resources (favorite pets, music, snack)

- Electronic & Standard Resources (calculators, pencil, note paper, erasers)

- Something else that helps you focus while working

Actions you may find helpful...

1. Some people feel the urge to physically move around while trying to concentrate on their work. Go ahead and move around.

2. If you have a favorite Fidget Toy or Object to hold in your hand to help you maintain your focus while working, feel free to use it.

3. Visual Objects you can touch and move around are fun resources when engaged in solving math problems. Buckets, bins or containers of buttons, dried kidney beans, dry pasta (uncooked) are helpful for counting and learning. So grab those, too.

Welcome to: The Budding Young Poets' Zone!

Dear _____ :
(Write your name here)

Welcome to your opportunity to become a Budding Young Poet!

As a Budding Young Poet you will learn poetry skills by creating fun rhyme scheme patterns. Developing rhyme schemes is done by putting words together in patterns to generate rhythm. But to make your experience even more enjoyable you have the opportunity to become the main character in the first several poems. For instance, Activity 1 invites you to replace the main characters with your name. In some poems, you will be invited to include others to join the cast of main characters.

Activities 2, 3, 4 and 5 not only include you and others you choose to be the main characters, you will learn one of the most fun and popular rhyme scheme patterns commonly used by many beginners interested in exploring poetry. Did you know most budding poets and rap artists began learning how to rap using a very common rhyme scheme known as the **AA, BB, CC** scheme? The poems gradually progress by using a variety of rhyme schemes; including **ABBA**, and other patterns. While rhyming patterns drive the creation of many of today's popular classics, hip hop, rap, spoken word and other well known contemporary artists are skilled at playing with words, also known as word craft. The art of developing messages through rhymes is a unique and fun experience. The poetry activities are designed to allow you to experience building word craft skills to develop your sense of rhyme and rhythm while also creating thoughtful messages. Learning by doing is the best way to learn anything new!

If you need support selecting words that rhyme, Word Banks are available for your use in all poems. Word Banks contain a random assortment of words, but only one will make sense and be the correct answer. So, read the list of words carefully and select the one that rhymes best with the last word in each sentence where you see (_____). You are also free to add your own words. Just be sure that whatever word you choose rhymes and fits the flow of the poem and be sure your answer makes sense!

My hope is you will discover and embrace your hidden creative talents. Wait...Who Got Goosed?™ Companion Activity Book was designed to inspire interest in poetry, math, and drawing through a range of emotions, including joy and laughter. Have fun!

Julie

Budding Young Poets' Table of Contents

Activity 1

Here is your chance to become the main character in each poem!
Just fill in the blanks using your name and pronouns.

Pronoun examples:
she/her, he/him, they/them (or another!)

Noun examples:
a person, place or thing

Possessive Pronoun examples:
mine, your, his, hers, its, theirs, ours

Adjective examples: (descriptive words)
beautiful, smooth, short, tall

- Little Laid Back Bo Peep (Little Bo Peep)
- Eensy Weensy Spider or Not! It's Still a Spider (Eensy Weensy Spider)
- Can You Imagine Jack Without Jill? (Jack and Jill)
- Old Innovative MacDonald (Old MacDonald)

Little Laid Back Bo Peep

_____ awoke this morning and discovered _____ has lost _____ sheep
(Your name)   (Your pronoun)   (Possessive pronoun)

And can't tell where to find them

_____ decided to leave them alone, hoping they'd come home
(Your name)

With their tails tucked behind them.

But after a day or two _____ felt like such a fool
(Your name)

'Cause the sheep continued to roam!

With their passports in order, they made for the Canadian border

They had no intention of returning home.

Filled with panic, the villagers sounded the alarm

But truly _____ intended to do no harm!
(Your name)

Just this once _____ hoped _____ could be forgiven for _____ mistake
(Your name)   (Your pronoun)   (Possessive pronoun)

A year ago, _____ lost cattle and was forgiven,
(Name and blame someone else)

so _____ pleaded, "Let it go for goodness sake!"
(Your name)

Eensy Weensy Spider or Not! It's Still a Spider

The Eensy Weensy Spider went up the <u>waterspout</u>.

When _____ noticed the spider, _____ panicked and gave a frantic <u>shout</u>!
(Your name)   (Pronoun)

Being afraid of spiders _____ entire <u>life</u>,
(Possessive pronoun)

_____ immediately ran as if in fear of losing _____ life
(Your name)   (Possessive pronoun)

You would have thought _____ was deeply wounded
(Your name)

by an accidental cut from a <u>knife</u>

Fueled with a fear of all spiders, before entering rooms _____ carefully inspects
(Your name)

every space <u>twice</u>!

Can You Imagine Jack Without Jill?

Jack and Jill never went up the <u>hill</u> —

It was _____ who fetched a pail of water and had a minor <u>spill</u>
(Your name or that of someone else)

You see, Jack and Jill are _____'s siblings, but too young to do <u>chores</u>
(Repeat name)

So _____ is stuck cleaning the _____ and fetching water while
(Repeat name)   (Noun - place or thing)

they play <u>outdoors</u>

On a few occasions while fetching water, _____ has fallen <u>down</u>
(Repeat name)

Twisting _____ ankle, which creates unwelcome and annoying chatter around <u>town</u>
(Possessive pronoun)

Some folks took pleasure in exaggerating _____'s minor <u>scrape</u>
(Repeat name)

Even the claims of _____ ankle not being in very good <u>shape</u>
(Possessive pronoun or noun)

Understandably, after reading those reports online, _____ is a bit <u>miffed</u>
(Repeat name)

Because false information shared anywhere is such an embarrassing <u>diss</u>

And with no way for _____ to erase those words and replace them with the <u>truth</u>
(Repeat name)

_____ discovered how hurtful words are and even more difficult to <u>refute</u>!
(Repeat name)

Wait a minute… this image was posted just yesterday! The entire thing is totally <u>fake</u>!

_____ put _____ phone down, and rejoined _____ family
(Repeat name)   (Possessive pronoun)   (Possessive pronoun)

Who was on vacation, relaxing at their favorite <u>lake</u>.

What is _____ **thinking? Fill in the thought bubble above!**
(Your name or that of someone else)

Old Innovative MacDonald

Old _____ has a farm
(Abbreviation or nickname that's short for MacDonald)

E-I-E-I-O

Every day _____ milks the cows, gets hay for the sheep
(Your name)

And tends to the crop of fruits and vegetables that grow

_____ lives next door to Old MacDonald
(Your name)

And is one of his favorite neighbors

So when needed, _____ chips in and helps with the chores
(Your name)

Whenever Old MacDonald needs a favor

The only downside to _____'s pitching in
(Your name)

Is having to wear knee-high rubber boots

'Cause slogging through the pigs' pen

Is never a hoot!

_____ has tried other ways to prevent inhaling the awful smell
(Your name)

Unfortunately clothesline clips, cotton balls, and other forms of protection haven't worked out well!

How _____ manages to get through so many unpleasant chores
(Your name)

Has to do with _____ enjoyment of living most of _____ life outdoors!
(Possessive pronoun)   (Possessive pronoun)

When asked by Old MacDonald, _____ is always available. Why?
(Your name)

Farming is laborious, but everyone loves being outside under open skies,

And living in a diverse community of farmers of every ethnicity,

Creates a genuine sense of community among people invested in making agriculture their specialty

Old MacDonald is the only farmer with a mega-sized pigs' pen

Which always makes that the speediest chore for _____ , who is naturally always in a
(Your name)

hurry to bring _____ time in the pen to a quick end
(Possessive pronoun)

Despite efforts to plead and beg siblings to just help _____ with that chore
(Your name)

There are never any willing volunteers cause the funk is just waaaayyyyy too much to endure!

Activity 2

Add your name and contribute to the poem; choose a word for the end of the second line of each stanza that rhymes with the last word in the first sentence to create an **AA, BB, CC** rhyme scheme.

(_____) indicates Young Poets are free to supply any end rhyme they wish from the box or create their own rhyme.

- Not Again Georgy! (Georgy Porgy)
- When Punch Punched Judy (Punch and Judy)
- The Downside of Going Uptown (The Kid Who Went to Town)

Not Again Georgy!

_____ enjoyed hanging out with Georgy Porgy puddin' pie
(Your name)

Who was wrongly accused of kissing girls and making them (_____)
                                                                    1

When the neighborhood boys came out to play

Georgy and _____ always ran (_____)
            (Your name)   2

Tired of being bullied, Georgy and _____ preferred to be left alone
                                           (Your name)

And formed a friendship after discovering their mutual passion for game apps on their (_____)
                                                                                          3

_____ and Georgy also have a thirst for fast food and drinks
(Your name)

Whenever one makes the thumbs up sign, the other one smiles and (_____)
                                                                      4

It was Georgy and _____'s sign to meet up after school to play
                        (Your name)

Focusing on their work was hard because anticipating what was to come was so (_____)
                                                                                  5

Problem was Georgy had to be home no later than five

Because his mama put him out and now he's living with his Aunt (_____)
                                                                    6

Word Bank		
shy	cry	lie
sway	stay	away
cone	shown	phones
winks	blinks	sinks
pay	slay	stay
my	by	Vie

When _____ Punched _____
(Character 1)   (Character 2)

_____ and _____
(Character 1)   (Character 2)

Fought over the last piece of _____ pie
(Name your favorite pie)

_____ became upset with _____
(Character 1)   (Character 2)

Stating, "You never share!" and _____ began to (_____)
(Character 1 pronoun)   1

Remember to choose a word for the end of the second line of each stanza that rhymes with the last word in the first sentence to create an **AA, BB, CC** rhyme scheme.

"Geez!" said _____
(Character 2)

"Go ahead and take it, but you're not being fair!"

_____ shrugged _____ shoulders
(Character 1)   (Character 1 possessive pronoun)

And gave a smug, victorious smile, as _____ sat pouting in the (_____)
(Character 2)   2

Annoyed by the smile, _____ sat at another table
(Character 2)

And watched TV to calm _____ and become more (_____)
(Character 2 personal pronoun + self)   3

After the last bite, _____ regretted not sharing the _____ pie
(Character 1)   (Name your favorite pie)

When _____ attempted to apologize, _____ discovered _____
(Character 1 pronoun)   (Character 1 pronoun)   (Character 2)

had already split without saying, "_____"
4

Word Bank		
pie	sly	cry
care	chair	hair
stable	able	table
tribe	cry	goodbye

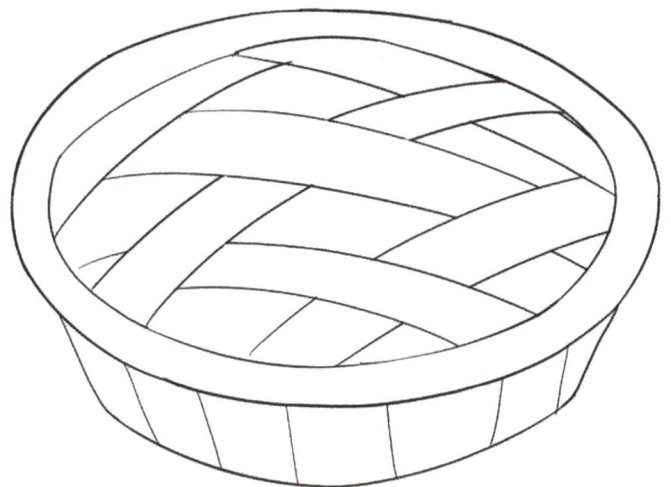

Add toppings to the pie or draw the ingredients on the counter that you'd need to make your favorite kind of pie!

The Downside of Going Uptown

When _____ was a little _____, about _____ years old
(Your name or the name of a boy, girl, person or child)   (Pronoun)   (Age)

_____ went shopping with _____ mama to buy new (_____)
(Chosen name)   (Possessive pronoun)   1

Tired of having _____ mama decide what to buy
(Possessive pronoun)

_____ came up with a plan _____ wasn't sure would work but gave it a
(Chosen name)   (Pronoun)

(_____)
2

_____ asked _____ mama for an allowance, but mama wasn't sure she
(Chosen name)   (Possessive pronoun)

heard what _____ said
(Chosen name)

_____ asked again and mama stared at _____ as if _____ had two
(Chosen name)   (Pronoun)   (Pronoun)

(_____)
3

Mama explained that she barely had enough money to put food on the table each day;

_____ froze and felt embarrassed, then began stuttering, unsure about what to
(Chosen name)

(_____)
4

But like other kids, _____ refused to give up and thought of a new plan;
(Chosen name)

Recalling how the last conversation went made _____ pause, unsure how the new
(Chosen name)

suggestion would (_____)
5

Asking, "What if I did chores for neighbors around the neighborhood?"

They could pay me for _____ or _____. Wouldn't that be
(Name a chore or task)   (Name a chore or task)

(_____)?"
6

Impressed with how enterprising _____ was, mama smiled and said she <u>approved</u>.
(Chosen name)

Then she stated, "You can start with weekly chores around the house, like the trash which needs to

be immediately (_____)."
7

Feeling euphoric, _____ excitedly asked, "Will I get paid each week for removing
(Chosen name)

the <u>trash</u>?"

_____ mama looked at _____ and began to (_____)
(Possessive pronoun)   (Personal pronoun)   8

Over the next year, _____ mowed lawns and removed <u>snow</u>
(Chosen name)

And became diligent about saving every dollar, taking pleasure in watching _____
(Possessive pronoun)

savings steadily (_____).
9

_____ was rewarded before the start of the next school <u>year</u>
(Chosen name)

_____ finally got to select and pay for _____ new clothes and cool
(Chosen name)   (Possessive pronoun)

(_____).
10

Anticipating the beginning of the new school year, was so much <u>fun</u>

Showing up in new clothes, eager to show _____
11

But the deed _____ did for _____ mama meant so much <u>more</u>
(Pronoun)   (Possessive pronoun)

The first time _____ helped pay the bills almost made mama fall to the (_____)
(Pronoun)   12

clothes	pose	knows	**Word Bank**
tie	cry	try	
said	heads	sleds	
hay	say	pay	
land	plan	sand	
could	good	should	
fooled	schooled	removed	
laugh	calf	staff	
show	toe	grow	
gear	cheer	deer	
some	none	everyone	
sore	floor	core	

Now's your chance to be a designer! Color in the dresses
to match the poem you just finished!

Activity 3

Insert your name or the name of a friend (instead of Taffy)
to complete the poem.

- What's Taffy Up To Now? (Taffy)

What's _____ Up To Now?
(Your name or the name of a friend)

_____ is my friend and <u>neighbor</u>
(Name from the poem's title)
Who is known for doing other people kind (_____)
                                                              1

After hearing someone stole a sizeable piece of <u>beef</u>

_____asked, "From whom?" so _____ could bring them (_____)
(Name from the poem's title)   (Personal pronoun)   2

Stealing from neighbors earning low incomes made it impossible to escape being <u>poor</u>

This did not sit well with _____, who thought it shameful
                                              (Name from the poem's title)
To take from others with low incomes making purchases they could barely (_____)!
                                                                                                        3

_____ had saved several weeks of _____ allowance, earned for
(Name from the poem's title)   (Possessive pronoun)
_____ at <u>home</u>,
(List one chore)

_____'s original plan was to use the money saved to buy new _____.
(Name from the poem's title)   4

Instead _____ went to the grocery store with a list of items including beef and
              (Name from the poem's title)

collard <u>greens</u>

Then _____ placed the bag of groceries at _____ neighbor's door.
         (Pronoun)   (Possessive pronoun)
Rang the doorbell, ran, and hid to avoid being (_____)
                                                                          5

Barely reaching the patch of _____ planted along the edge of _____
(Name of a favorite flower or plant)   (Possessive pronoun)

neighbor's <u>tree</u>

_____ felt immense pleasure in seeing her neighbor's reaction;
(Name from the poem's title)

And _____ thought about more acts of kindness towards others living in _____.
(Pronoun)   6

Because _____ didn't have a real job, acts of giving would need to be spread <u>out</u>
(Name from the poem's title)

But _____ discovered time and money didn't really matter
(Name from the poem's title)

When doing good deeds for others in need was really what it was all _____.
7

Much to _____'s surprise, _____ good deeds became known
(Name from the poem's title)   (Possessive pronoun)

throughout the <u>neighborhood</u>

Family and friends inquired how _____ was able to fund the acts of kindness
(Name from the poem's title)

and other generous deeds intended to do so much (_____)
5

Word Bank		
flavors	savor	favors
relief	chief	belief
sword	record	afford
cones	shown	headphones
mean	seen	clean
anxiety	poverty	sloppy
spout	snout	about
good	wood	would

Activity 4

Finish the poem.

- See See (See See)

See See

See, see! What shall I <u>see</u>?

Look way up above the (_____)
1

And just watch the clouds in the <u>sky</u>

Okay, you may ask, but (_____)?
2

'Cause clouds aren't just clouds bringing <u>rain</u>,

They're majestic! Like paintings in motion without a picture (_____)
3

The movement of clouds is like a free art <u>show</u>

Moving fast or moving slow. It's quite beautiful to watch the formations come and (_____)!
4

Word Bank		
please	trees	knees
why	shy	bye
same	frame	came
sew	slow	go

Activity 5

Use rhymes to tell the story of a day in the life of a family.

- One Two, Buckle My Shoe

One Two, Buckle My Shoe

One, two

Has anybody seen my other _____ (_____)?

(Adjective or describing word)   1

Three, four

When leaving for school, mom and dad both yelled, "Don't forget to _____, and

(Something parents ask you to do)

please don't slam the (_____)

     2

Five, six

My dog Sugahbear jumped and gave me a _____ (_____)

(Describing word)   3

Seven, eight

During breakfast, begged my parents to let me play _____ and stay up

(Name a fun game)

(_____)

4

Nine, ten

"If it was a weekend night," they said, "we could let you play and allow the rule to (_____)

     5

Eleven, twelve

Which meant "No!" They just want the topic dropped 'cause they're only thinking of (_____)

     6

Thirteen, <u>fourteen</u>

I put on a pouty look, which was my way of making a (_____)
7

Fifteen, <u>sixteen</u>

But that never works. Seriously, sometimes parents are just so (_____)!
8

Seventeen, <u>eighteen</u>

I sat at the back of the school bus, which is _____ and (_____)
(Adjective)   9

Nineteen, <u>twenty</u>

My friends saw I was in a _____ mood, which they found (_____)
(Adjective or describing word)   10

Twenty-one, <u>twenty-two</u>

I really felt _____ and wasn't sure what to (_____)
(Emotion or feeling)   11

Twenty-three and <u>four</u>

When I got home, I expressed _____ by slamming the front (_____)
(A feeling noun, a mood or emotion)   12

Twenty-five and <u>six</u>

Then I accidentally blurted out loud, "Sometimes you make me (_____)!"
13

Twenty-seven and <u>eight</u>

Mama said, "Since you're not feeling well, looks like you won't be able to stay up (_____)!"
14

Twenty-nine and <u>thirty</u> (your turn....finish this poem any way you prefer! How many more stanzas can you create?)

_____

_____

_____

_____

_____

_____

_____

_____

_____

_____

Word Bank		
do	shoe	chew
door	more	floor
miss	dish	licks
gate	great	late
end	bend	send
themselves	elves	shelves
sheen	bean	scene
green	mean	seen
keen	unclean	screen
sunny	honey	funny
do	fool	cool
door	before	floor
nick	slick	sick
snake	late	great

Welcome to: The Budding Young Math Wizards' Zone!

Greetings Budding Math Wizards!

Welcome to a series of fun and engaging math brain teasers that need your wizard's skills to solve them. Every math problem is linked with characters in the Wait...Who Got Goosed?™ poems. For example, your math wizards skills are needed to help them figure out how much money will be lost if these sheep are not returned. And passports to cross the Canadian border are not cheap. So put on your wizard's thinking cap, and grab the resources you may need to to help you solve mathematical mysteries. *And oh . . . have fun.*

Your task: Solve the mystifying brain teasers for the following poems:
- Eensy Weensy Spider or Not! It's Still a Spider (Eensy Weensy Spider)
- Not Again Georgy! (Georgy Porgy)
- Can You Imagine Jack Without Jill? (Jack and Jill)
- Old Innovative MacDonald (Old MacDonald)
- Mary's Loyal Lil Lamb (Mary Had A Little Lamb)

GRADE LEVEL KEY:

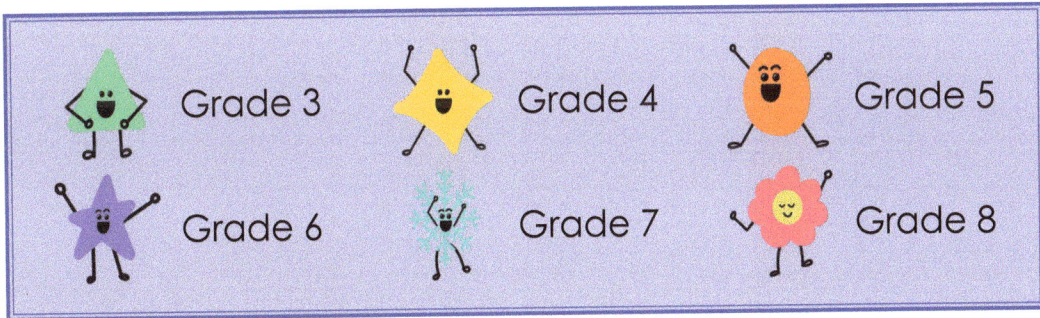

What's A Grade Level Key and What Is Its Purpose?

- Each Symbol in the Grade Level Key box represents a specific grade
- Symbols are placed next to math problems
- If you are in the third grade your symbol is
- Every question with a   next to it is for math wizards at the 3rd grade level
- Everyone is welcome to tackle each problem, so go ahead and solve all or as many as you wish!

Keys to success:

1. Give each problem your best effort!

2. Try to identify what the question is asking.

3. What key words and numbers will you need to solve the problem?

4. Are there other facts that might help you solve the problem?

5. Is there a diagram or a formula you can create to help solve the problem?

6. Show the steps you are thinking to help solve the problem. (Show your work.)

7. Review your work to make sure it answers the question.

8. It's often helpful to break problems into small steps when needed to solve them.

Don't worry! You've got this!

By the end of your journey you may be surprised by how much math you know.

Welcome to the Budding Math Wizards' Zone

TASK: SOLVE THE MYSTIFYING BRAIN TEASERS FOR THE FOLLOWING POEMS

1. Eensy Weensy Spider or Not! It's Still a Spider (Eensy Weensy Spider)
2. Not Again Georgy! (Georgy Porgy)
3. Can You Imagine Jack Without Jill? (Jack and Jill)
4. Old Innovative MacDonald (Old MacDonald)
5. Mary's Loyal Lil Lamb (Mary Had A Little Lamb)

Eensy Weensy Spider or Not! It's Still a Spider

The Ensee Weensy Spider went up the waterspout.

My mama was washing the dishes when I heard a frantic shout.

That Ensee Weensy Spider must have been taken by surprise.

But in no way did it compare to the panic in mama's eyes.

She yelled, "There's a spider in the sink!"

I glanced at the spider, and it gave me a wink.

So I let that spider retreat and hide in the spout,

Cause my mama looked so funny, I enjoyed anticipating another round of frantic shouts.

 # Question 1

Multiple Choice: How many legs does a spider have? (Use the picture to help you or draw one of your own.)

A. 2 legs

B. 4 legs

C. 8 legs

D. 16 legs

 # Question 2

How many total legs do two spiders have?

 # Question 3

How many total legs do five spiders have?

 # Question 4

If there are a total of 64 legs, how many spiders are there?

 # Question 5

If the mama was washing the dishes for 15 minutes before the spider appeared, and the spider hid for 5 minutes, how many minutes in total was the mama washing dishes?

 # Question 6

If the mama shouted in panic for 20 seconds, and the spider hid for 10 seconds, how many seconds of panic did the mama experience in total?

 # Question 7

If the Ensee Weensy Spider went up the waterspout at 2:00 PM and the mama started washing dishes at 1:30 PM, how long had the mama been washing dishes before encountering the spider?

 # Question 8

Multiple Choice: If a pair means two, how many pairs of legs does one spider have?

   A. 2 pairs of legs

   B. 4 pairs of legs

   C. 8 pairs of legs

   D. 16 pairs of legs

 # Question 9

How many pairs of legs do four spiders have?

 # Question 10

If the Ensee Weensy Spider has 8 legs and each leg has 7 segments, how many segments does a spider have in total?

 # Question 11

If the Ensee Weensy Spider went up the waterspout at a speed of 1 inch per second and it reached the top after 10 seconds, how tall was the waterspout?

 # Question 12

How many pairs of legs do ten spiders have?

 # Question 13

If the mama's frantic shout was 120 decibels and it echoed off the walls at 90 decibels, how much louder was mama's shout compared to the echo?

 # Question 14

If the mama started washing dishes at 1:30 PM and the spider was encountered at 1:45 PM, how many minutes did mama wash the dishes before seeing the spider?

 # Question 15

If there are a total of 400 pairs of legs, how many spiders are there in total?

 # Question 16

If the Ensee Weensy Spider went up the waterspout at a speed of 0.5 inches per second and it reached the top after 10 seconds, how tall was the waterspout?

Question 17

If mama saw the spider and shouted in panic for 20 seconds, and then spent 5 minutes trying to catch the spider, how many seconds did she spend in total interacting with the spider?

Question 18

If mama started washing dishes at 1:30 PM and first saw the spider at 1:45 PM, how many seconds did it take for the spider to appear?

Question 19

Brain Teaser: How many spiders might there be if there are 38 total spider legs? Explain your reasoning.

Question 20

If mama shouted in panic for 20 seconds, and she repeatedly shouted 5 more times, how many seconds did she spend shouting in total?

Not Again Georgy!

Georgy Porgy puddin pie

Kissed the girls and made them cry

When the boys came out to play

Georgy Porgy always ran away

While strolling towards home

He felt sad and very alone

When without warning out of a big oak tree

Came a swarm of buzzing bees

Georgy knew he had to think fast

Desperate to not get stung he ran into oncoming traffic under an overpass

He ran all the way home, and was out of breath

His mama glared at him and said, "I see you've gotten yourself into another mess"

© 2024 Julie Coles | *Wait...Who Got Goosed?*™ Activity Book

"Yesterday you were pestering the girls over near the Martin's place

You're in trouble boy, I can see fear written on your face"

Georgy Porgy tried, in vain, to explain

His mama said, "Whatever it is, I know you're to blame

I got a call from Sara's mom and she sounded so miffed

She claims you chased her girl. Did you ask her for a kiss?"

"I've warned you before, boy you'd better cut that out."

And in a thunderous voice she began to shout

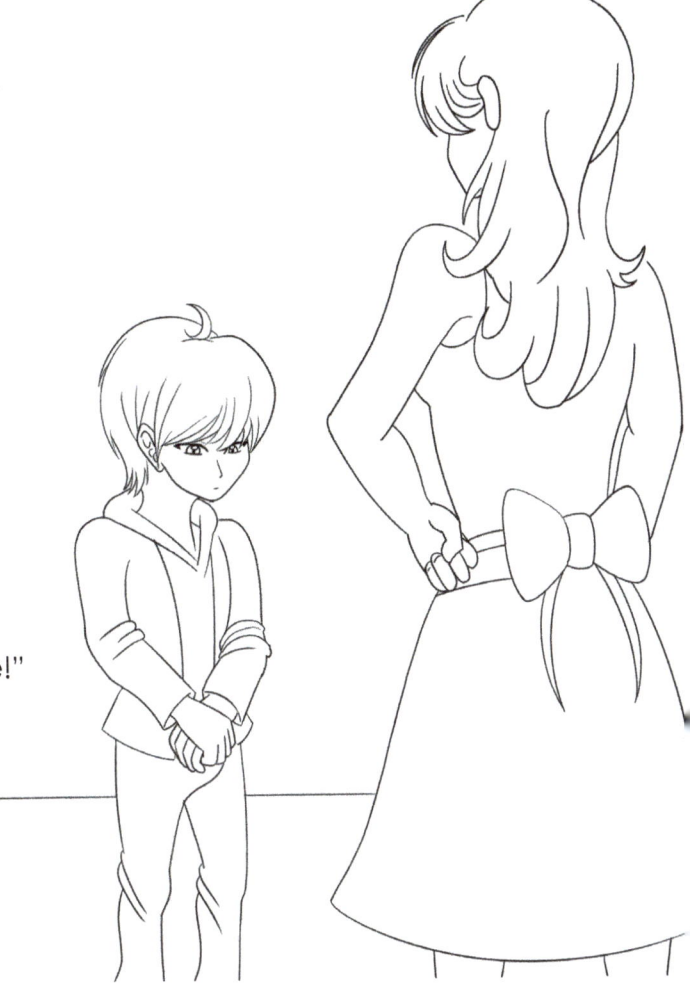

"Georgy Porgy puddin pie

If you even attempt to touch one more girl

You can pack your clothes and go live with your Aunt Vie!"

 ## Question 1

If Georgy Porgy always ran away when the boys came out to play, and they played 3 times a week, how many times did he run away in a month?

 ## Question 2

If Georgy Porgy felt sad and very alone for 30 minutes, how many hours was he sad?

 ## Question 3

If Georgy Porgy pestered the girls near the Martin's place for 4 days, and each day he bothered them for 20 minutes, how many minutes did he spend bothering the girls in total?

 ## Question 4

If Aunt Vie lives 75 miles away, and Georgy Porgy has to pack his clothes to go live with her, how many miles will he travel?

 Question 5

If Georgy Porgy ran for 3 blocks, and each block is 150 feet long, how many feet did he run?

 Question 6

If Georgy Porgy ran for 25 minutes to get all the way home and was out of breath, what was his average speed if he covered 5 miles?

 Question 7

If Georgy Porgy ran for 2 hours and covered a distance of 8 miles, what was his average speed?

 Question 8

If Georgy Porgy received 3 warnings from his mama, and each warning took 6 minutes to deliver, how much time did he spend being warned?

 # Question 9

If Aunt Vie's house is 120 miles away, and Georgy Porgy travels at an average speed of 60 miles per hour, how long will it take him to reach Aunt Vie's house?

 # Question 10

If Georgy Porgy ran for 2 hours and 30 minutes, and each hour he covered 3 miles, how far did he run in total?

 # Question 11

If Georgy Porgy received a call from Sara's mom at 4:15 PM and the call lasted 10 minutes, at what time did he finish the call?

 # Question 12

If Georgy Porgy attempted to explain himself for 20 minutes but his mama didn't believe him, and she shouted for 10 minutes, how long did the entire interaction take?

 # Question 13

If Georgy Porgy's mama shouted for 20% of the time she was talking to him, and the entire conversation took 30 minutes, how many minutes did she shout?

 # Question 14

If the boys came out to play 5 times each week and Georgy Porgy ran away from the boys every time they came out to play for 4 months, how many times did he run away in total?

 # Question 15

If Georgy Porgy ran for 2 hours and 30 minutes, and each minute he covered 100 yards, how far did he run?

 # Question 16

If Georgy Porgy pestered the girls near the Martin's place for 3 days and chased them for 2 hours each day, how many hours did he spend bothering the girls in total?

 **Question 17**

If the buzzing bees came out of the big oak tree for 10 seconds, and there were 5 bees that flew out per second, how many bees were in the swarm?

 **Question 18**

If Georgy Porgy ran away from oncoming traffic for 5 minutes, and he ran at an average speed of 3 miles per hour, how far did he run?

 **Question 19**

If Georgy Porgy ran for 2 hours and 30 minutes, and each hour he covered 5 kilometers, how far did he run in total?

Can You Imagine Jack Without Jill?

Jack and Jill went up the hill

To fetch a pail of water

Jack fell down and broke his crown

And now he's lying up at City Hospital

Taped in bandages from head to toe

When the family can expect him to be released

The doctors really don't know

After Jack fell down and broke his crown

They say Jill came tumbling after

She's not in bad shape

Just a few minor scrapes

But she's in no mood for laughter

Upon hearing news of Jack's uncertain day of release

Jill was filled with so much anguish and alarm

She hated the thought of doing the chores alone

Her hands swelled with pain throbbing down to the bone

Her parents seemed unconcerned about the injury to her arm

Understandably Jill is upset

Knowing she'll eventually recover and resume fetching the water alone.

Her foul demeanor began to ratchet up a bit more

Roaming through the house and slamming doors

And calls from the hospital infuriated her so much she refused to pick up the phone

When learning that Jack needed additional time to heal,

Jill grew suspicious that Jack may be faking his pain

So her anger grew with daily temper-tantrums and escalating outbursts

Her parents started hearing threats of boycotts and being left to die of thirst

Clearly Jill was becoming unhinged and maybe a bit insane

Determined to use this moment to her advantage

Knowing a home without water would just never do

Jill researched available options based on what her family could afford

Five days later they found a red wagon with bottles of water at their front door

But Jill knew more needed to be done to make certain her parents were aware her days of fetching

water were through

She boldly announced that when Jack returns to good health he can start fetching the water alone

And reminded her parents she wasn't kidding, threatening, "If I have to fetch one more pail of water

I'm running away from home!"

 ## Question 1

If Jill refuses to pick up the phone because she is so angry, and the phone rings every 15 minutes, how many times does the phone ring in an hour?

 ## Question 2

If Jill's foul demeanor escalates, and she slams doors every 10 minutes, how many doors does she slam in 1 hour?

 ## Question 3

If Jill receives a red wagon with bottles of water every 2 days, how many wagons will she receive in a week?

 ## Question 4

If Jill is in pain for 4 days and each day she fetches water for 30 minutes, how many minutes does she spend in pain fetching water?

 # Question 5

If Jill receives a red wagon with 10 bottles of water, and each bottle contains 500 milliliters, how many milliliters of water does she receive?

 # Question 6

If Jill's parents hear threats of boycotts every 20 minutes, and they continue for an hour, how many threats do they hear?

 # Question 7

If Jill refuses to get water for 3 days, and the family needs 2 liters of water per day, how many liters of water do they need in total for the days Jill did not get water?

 # Question 8

If Jill's parents are aware her days of fetching water are through and they drink 1 liter of water every 2 hours, how many liters do they drink in 10 hours?

 ## Question 9

If Jill spends 2 days without sleep worrying about Jack's release, and she checks for updates every 30 minutes, how many times does she check for updates in total?

 ## Question 10

If Jack needs additional time to heal and Jill grows suspicious, and she checks his temperature every 4 hours, how many times does she check in a day?

 ## Question 11

If Jill's anger grows with daily temper tantrums, and she has 3 tantrums a day, how many tantrums does she have in a week?

 ## Question 12

If Jill fetches water twice a day and spends 40 minutes each time, how many minutes does she spend fetching water in a week?

 **Question 13**

If Jill fetches water for 4 days and each day she fetches 2 pails of water, how many pails does she fetch in total?

 **Question 14**

If Jill receives a red wagon with 10 bottles of water every 3 days, and she drinks 2 bottles a day, how many bottles does she have left at the end of the week?

 **Question 15**

If Jill refuses to pick up the phone for 2 days and the phone rings every 10 minutes, how many calls does she miss?

 **Question 16**

If Jill receives a red wagon with 10 bottles of water every 3 days, and she drinks 2 bottles a day, how many bottles does she receive in a month?

 # Question 17

If Jill's parents are left to die of thirst for 3 days, and each day they need 1.5 liters of water, how many liters of water does Jill need to provide to save them?

 # Question 18

If Jill fetches water twice a day and spends 45 minutes each time, and she fetches water for 5 days, how many hours does she spend fetching water in total?

 # Question 19

If Jill fetches water twice a day and announces she will run away from home if she has to fetch one more pail of water, and she runs away after 20 days, how many times does she fetch water before leaving?

Old Innovative MacDonald
(Put some respect on his name!)

Old MacDonald has a farm

E I E I O

I was given directions to this mysterious place

But I'm not sure I'm gonna go

Even though I am rather curious

His farm is kind of far

And good directions don't matter

If you don't have a dependable car

Gosh, I'm so torn about this trip

Cause his place has such a reputation

Traffic gets backed up for miles

Visitors eager to see cows rumored to be a singing sensation

Imagine animals putting on a musical show

With altos and sopranos all singing in key

Belting out songs Mac taught them

In perfect harmony

Did you know their tunes are so popular

They were invited to the Grammys to sing their biggest hit?

Apparently they tend to poop while singing

Panicking dignitaries, scattering to find somewhere else to sit

Old MacDonald's farm may smell a bit funky

Most visitors plug their noses while passing through

But as unpleasant as folks may find the odor

I hear sessions are sold out every afternoon at two

 # Question 1

If Old MacDonald's farm is a bit far and it takes 2 hours to drive there, how many hours will it take to drive round trip?

 # Question 2

If visitors are eager to see cows rumored to be a singing sensation and each visitor pays $5 for entry, how much money does Old MacDonald make if 20 visitors come?

 # Question 3

If musical shows at Old MacDonald's farm are sold out every afternoon at 2 PM and each session lasts 1 hour, how many hours of shows are there in a week?

 # Question 4

If the animals at Old MacDonald's farm sing their biggest hit for 15 minutes, and they sing it three times a day, how many minutes do they sing it in a day?

 **Question 5**

If Old MacDonald's farm has 10 cows and each cow produces 5 gallons of milk a day, how many gallons of milk do they produce in total in one day?

 **Question 6**

If visitors are eager to see cows rumored to be a singing sensation and each visitor pays $5 for entry, how much money does Old MacDonald make if 50 visitors come?

 **Question 7**

If Old MacDonald's farm has 10 cows and each cow produces 5 gallons of milk a day, how many total gallons of milk do they produce in a week?

 **Question 8**

If sessions at Old MacDonald's farm are sold out every afternoon at 2 PM and each session can accommodate 30 visitors, how many visitors attend the sessions in a week?

 **Question 9**

If Old MacDonald's farm has 20 visitors each day, and each visitor brings 2 children with them, how many people visit the farm in a week?

 **Question 10**

If Old MacDonald's farm has 10 cows and each cow produces 5 gallons of milk a day, how many gallons of milk do they produce in a month?

 **Question 11**

If visitors are eager to see cows rumored to be a singing sensation and each visitor pays $5 for entry, how much money does Old MacDonald make if 100 visitors come?

 **Question 12**

If the animals at Old MacDonald's farm sing their biggest hit for 15 minutes, and they sing it every hour for four hours each day, how many hours do they spend singing in a week?

 # Question 13

If Old MacDonald's farm has 20 visitors each day, and each visitor brings 2 children with them, how many people visit the farm in a month?

 # Question 14

If Old MacDonald's farm has 10 cows and each cow produces 5 gallons of milk a day, how many gallons of milk do they produce in a year?

 # Question 15

If visitors are eager to see cows rumored to be a singing sensation and each visitor pays $5 for entry, how much money does Old MacDonald make if 450 visitors come?

 # Question 16

If the animals at Old MacDonald's farm sing their biggest hit for 15 minutes, and they sing it every hour, how many hours do they spend singing in a day?

 **Question 17**

If sessions at Old MacDonald's farm are sold out every afternoon at 2 PM and each session can accommodate 30 visitors, how many visitors attend the sessions in a year?

 **Question 18**

If Old MacDonald's farm has 20 visitors each day, and each visitor brings 2 children with them, how many people visit the farm in a year?

 **Question 19**

If Old MacDonald's farm has 10 cows and each cow produces 5 gallons of milk a day, how many gallons of milk do they produce in 5 years?

 **Question 20**

If visitors are eager to see cows rumored to be a singing sensation and each visitor pays $5 for entry, how much money does Old MacDonald make if 1,225 visitors come?

 # Question 21

If the animals at Old MacDonald's farm sing their biggest hit for 15 minutes, and they sing it every hour, how many hours do they spend singing in a year?

 # Question 22

If sessions at Old MacDonald's farm are sold out every afternoon at 2 PM and each session can accommodate 30 visitors, how many sessions are there in 5 years?

 # Question 23

If Old MacDonald's farm has 20 visitors each day, and each visitor brings 2 children with them, how many people visit the farm in 5 years?

 # Question 24

If Old MacDonald's farm has 10 cows and each cow produces 5 gallons of milk a day, how many gallons of milk do they produce in 10 years?

 # Question 25

If visitors are eager to see cows rumored to be a singing sensation and each visitor pays $5 for entry, how much money does Old MacDonald make if 2015 visitors come?

 # Question 26

If the animals at Old MacDonald's farm sing their biggest hit for 15 minutes, and they sing it every hour, how many hours do they spend singing in 10 years?

 # Question 27

If sessions at Old MacDonald's farm are sold out every afternoon at 2 PM and each session can accommodate 30 visitors, how many visitors attend the sessions in 10 years?

 # Question 28

If Old MacDonald's farm has 20 visitors each day, and each visitor brings 2 children with them, how many people visit the farm in 10 years?

Mary's Loyal Lil Lamb

Mary has a little lamb

His fleece as white as snow.

And everywhere that Mary goes,

That lamb is sure to go

He follows her to school

And her weekly aerobics class

But is reluctant about visits to the bank

Because the service there is never fast

Mary's lamb is so loyal

He even accompanies her to a dental appointment.

There is no deterring this little fella

His hoofs get so dry from long walks they usually require ointment

One day while filing her nails,

Mary began chatting while the lamb sat quietly beside her,

Said something about her class going on a field trip.

The news made his tail whip in excitement, causing him to shed his baby fur

So eager to plan his agenda for the day, he perked up his ears

Hearing something about visiting a farm where they shear sheep

Didn't raise any alarm for concern

But he wondered, "What the heck are shears?" as he bed down for the night to go to sleep

Now Mary has a lil' loyal lamb

Whose fleece was once white as snow

Sitting completely hairless and shivering in the corner, meekly asking,

"Ahh, about your plans for tomorrow? Do you think I oughta go?"

 # Question 1

If Mary's lamb accompanies her to school 5 days a week, how many times does the lamb go to school in a month?

 # Question 2

If Mary's lamb sheds its baby fur in 1 week, how many days does it take for the lamb to shed its fur?

 # Question 3

If Mary's lamb requires ointment for its hooves every 3 days, how many times does it need ointment in 2 weeks?

 # Question 4

If Mary's lamb sits quietly beside her for 10 minutes while she files her nails, and she files her nails every day, how many minutes does the lamb spend beside her in a week?

 **Question 5**

If Mary's lamb follows her to her weekly aerobics class and the class lasts for 1 hour, how many hours does the lamb spend at aerobics class in a month?

 **Question 6**

If Mary's lamb requires ointment for its hooves every 3 days, and a bottle of ointment lasts for 15 days, how many bottles of ointment does the lamb need in 2 months?

 **Question 7**

If Mary's lamb follows her to her weekly aerobics class and the class lasts for 1 hour, how many hours does the lamb spend at aerobics class in a year?

 **Question 8**

If Mary's lamb sheds its fur in 1 week, and it takes 2 weeks for the fur to grow back, how often does the lamb shed its fur in 6 months?

© 2024 Julie Coles | *Wait...Who Got Goosed?*™ Activity Book

 **Question 9**

If Mary's lamb sits quietly beside her for 10 minutes while she files her nails, and she files her nails every day, how many minutes does the lamb spend beside her in a year?

 **Question 10**

If Mary's lamb accompanies her to school 5 days a week, and there are 4 weeks in a month, how many days does the lamb go to school in 3 months?

 **Question 11**

If Mary's lamb requires ointment for its hooves every 3 days, and a bottle of ointment costs $10 and lasts for 15 days, how much money does Mary spend on ointment in a year?

 **Question 12**

If Mary's lamb follows her to her weekly aerobics class and the class lasts for 1 hour, how many hours does the lamb spend at aerobics class in 2 years?

 # Question 13

If Mary's lamb sheds its fur in 1 week, and it takes 2 weeks for the fur to grow back, how often does the lamb shed its fur in a year?

 # Question 14

If Mary's lamb sits quietly beside her for 10 minutes while she files her nails, and she files her nails every day, how many hours does the lamb spend beside her in a year?

 # Question 15

If Mary's lamb accompanies her to school 5 days a week, how many days does the lamb go to school in 2 years?

 # Question 16

If Mary's lamb requires ointment for its hooves every 3 days, and a bottle of ointment costs $12 and lasts for 15 days, how much money does Mary spend on ointment in 2 years?

 # Question 17

If Mary's lamb follows her to her weekly aerobics class and the class lasts for 1 hour, how many days does the lamb spend at aerobics class in 5 years?

 # Question 18

If Mary's lamb sheds its fur in 1 week, and it takes 2 weeks for the fur to grow back, how often does the lamb shed its fur in 10 years?

 # Question 19

If Mary's lamb sits quietly beside her for 10 minutes while she files her nails, and she files her nails every day, how many hours does the lamb spend beside her in 10 years?

 # Question 20

If Mary's lamb accompanies her to school 5 days a week, how many days does the lamb go to school in 5 years?

 # Question 21

If Mary's lamb requires ointment for its hooves every 3 days, and a bottle of ointment costs $10 and lasts for 15 days, how much money does Mary spend on ointment in 10 years?

 # Question 22

If Mary's lamb follows her to her weekly aerobics class and the class lasts for 1 hour, how many days does the lamb spend at aerobics class in 20 years?

 # Question 23

If Mary's lamb sheds its baby fur in 1 week, and it takes 2 weeks for the fur to grow back, how often does the lamb shed its fur in 20 years?

 # Question 24

If Mary's lamb sits quietly beside her for 10 minutes while she files her nails, and she files her nails every day, how many days does the lamb spend beside her in 20 years?

 # Question 25

If Mary's lamb accompanies her to school 5 days a week, how many days does the lamb go to school in 10 years?

 # Question 26

If Mary's lamb requires ointment for its hooves every 3 days, and a bottle of ointment costs $10 and lasts for 15 days, how much money does Mary spend on ointment in 20 years?

 # Question 27

If Mary's lamb follows her to her weekly aerobics class and the class lasts for 1 hour, how many hours does the lamb spend at aerobics class in 50 years?

 # Question 28

If Mary's lamb sheds its baby fur in 1 week, and it takes 2 weeks for the fur to grow back, how often does the lamb shed its fur in 50 years?

 **Question 29**

If Mary's lamb sits quietly beside her for 10 minutes while she files her nails, and she files her nails every day, how many hours does the lamb spend beside her in 50 years?

 **Question 30**

If Mary's lamb accompanies her to school 5 days a week, how many days does the lamb go to school in 50 years?

Additional Space to Work!

Welcome to: The Budding Young Artists' Zone!

Dear Artists!

Whether or not you have an interest in being a future artist, the Budding Young Artists' Zone is an open invitation to you to freely express yourself in colorful ways. Pick and choose images that appeal to you and color away! Different images may inspire you to use a color pencil instead of a crayon. Or you may want to design your own glamorous outfits for characters by cutting and pasting vivid images from magazines and fabric. If you have the digital copy of the activity book, then you have access to a selection of technology tools to support your artistic imagination.

Each picture is an open invitation for you to do as you wish. The real purpose of the coloring activity is to just allow you to have a joyful experience, without worrying about drawing outside the lines. You can even pretend the lines don't exist! Or you can remake your own version of each picture. For example, if you added wings to Bo Peep, she could fly away and escape being responsible for losing the village sheep. So, grab all the resources you need or want to use for the coloring book pages designed to welcome your artistic palette!

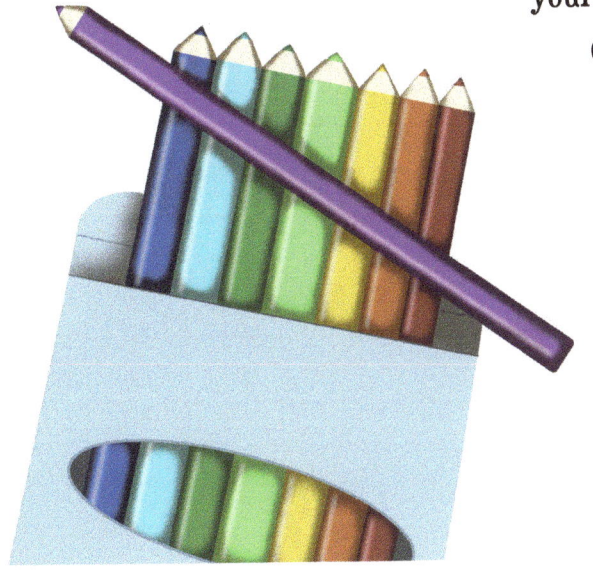

Bedtime Is A Nightmare

Doggone Shame

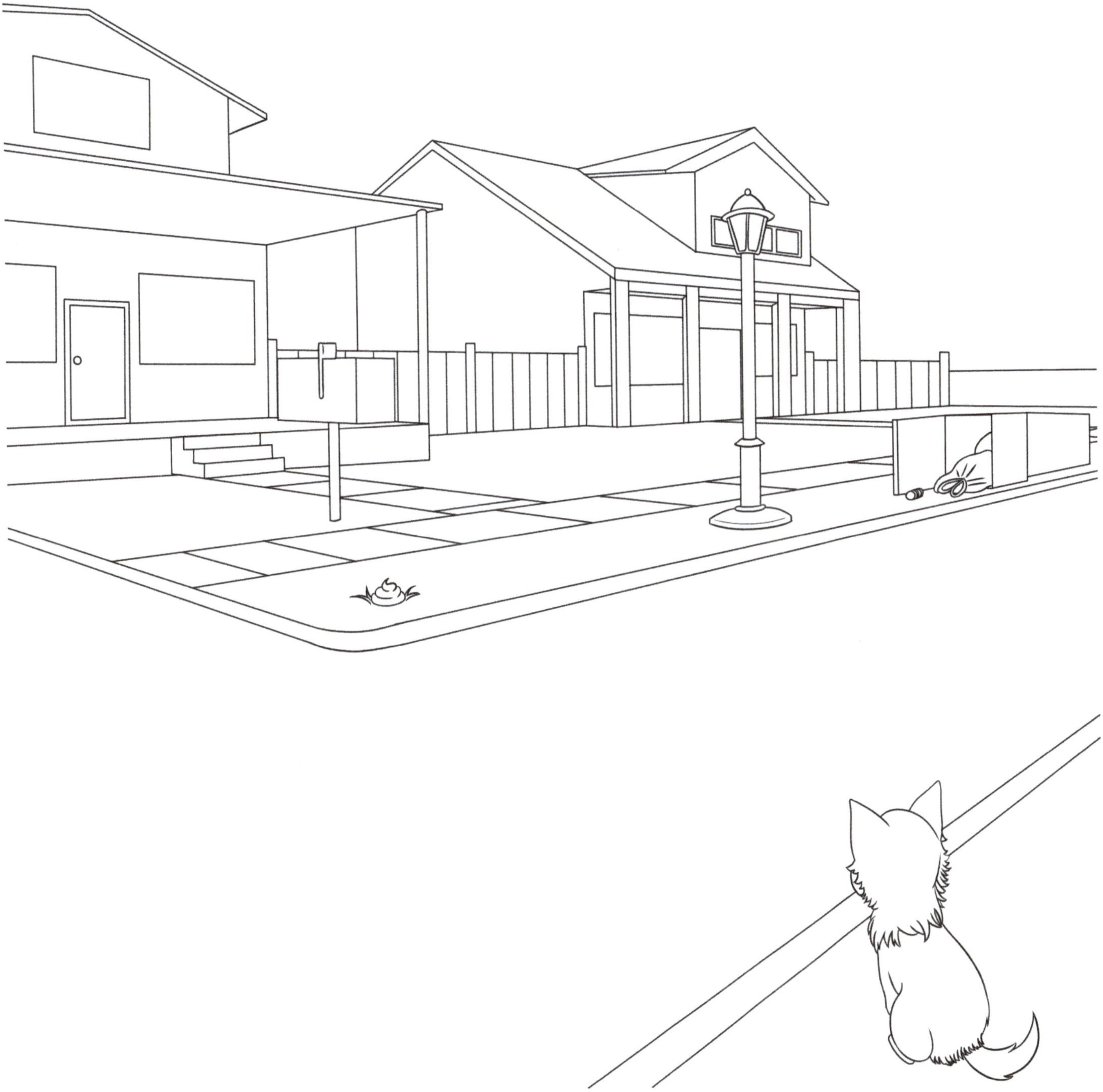

Tipsy Humpty Gets Dumptied

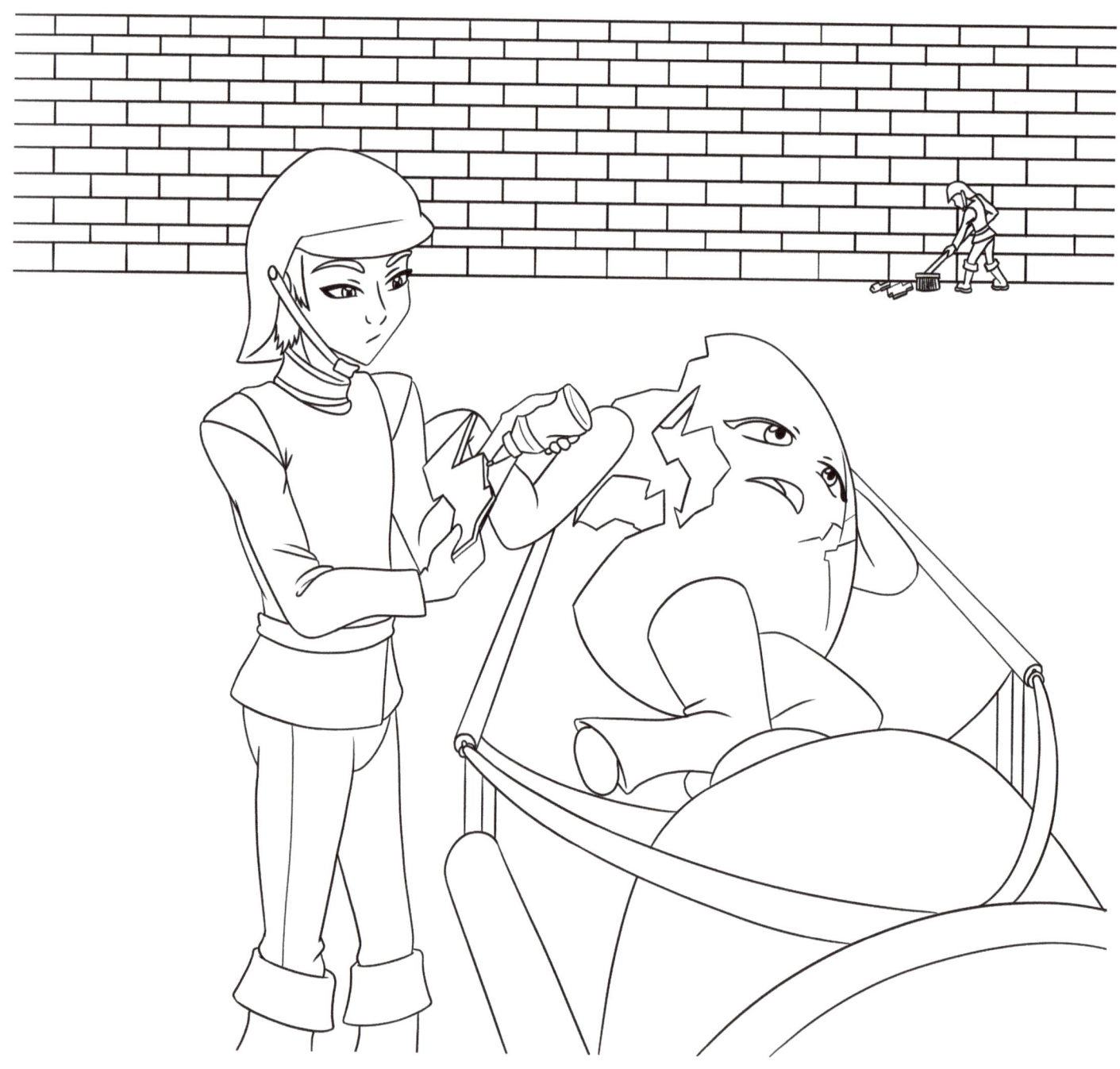

Jack's New Jingle

Little Tee Wee's Big Adventure At Sea

Mary's Loyal Lil' Lamb

Little Laid Back Bo Peep

Simon's Accidental Encounter

Three Cats of Kilkenny Are One Too Many

Whooo Should Listen to Wise Old Owls?

Old Innovative MacDonald (Put some respect on his name!)

Three Jive Mice

The Downside of Going Uptown

Ms. Muffet's Chill Time Interrupted

Welcome to: The Answer Key!

Poets' Activity 2
Not Again Georgy!

Correct Answer	Words That Rhyme, But Don't Quite Fit	
cry	shy	lie
away	stay	sway
phones	shown	cone
winks	blinks	sinks
slay	pay	stay
Vie	my	by

Poets' Activity 2
When Punch Punched Judy

Correct Answer	Words That Rhyme, But Don't Quite Fit	
cry	sly	pie
chair	care	hair
stable	able	table
goodbye	tribe	cry

Poets' Activity 2
The Downside of Going Uptown

Correct Answer	Words That Rhyme, But Don't Quite Fit	
clothes	knows	pose
try	tie	cry
heads	said	sleds
say	pay	hay
land	sand	plan
good	should	could
removed	fooled	schooled
laugh	staff	calf
grow	toe	show
gear	cheer	deer
some	none	everyone
floor	sore	core

Poets' Activity 3
What's _____ Up To Now?

Correct Answer	Words That Rhyme, But Don't Quite Fit	
favors	flavors	savor
relief	belief	chief
afford	record	sword
headphones	cones	shown
seen	clean	mean
poverty	anxiety	sloppy
about	snout	spout
good	wood	would

Poets' Activity 4
See See

Correct Answer	Words That Rhyme, But Don't Quite Fit	
trees	please	knees
why	shy	bye
frame	same	came
go	slow	sew

Poets' Activity 5
One Two, Buckle My Shoe

Correct Answer	Words That Rhyme, But Don't Quite Fit	
shoe	chew	do
door	floor	more
licks	dish	miss
late	great	gate
bend	send	end
themselves	shelves	elves
scene	bean	sheen
mean	seen	green
unclean	screen	keen
funny	honey	sunny
do	fool	cool
door	floor	before
sick	slick	nick
late	great	snake

Math Wizards'
Eensy Weensy Spider or Not! It's Still a Spider

1. C. 8 legs
2. 16 legs
3. 40 legs
4. 8 spiders
5. 20 minutes
6. 30 seconds
7. 30 minutes
8. B. 4 pairs of legs
9. 16 pairs of legs
10. 56 segments
11. 10 inches
12. 40 pairs of legs
13. 30 decibels
14. 15 minutes
15. 100 spiders
16. 5 inches
17. 320 seconds
18. 900 seconds
19. Answers vary. Possible answer: 5 spiders and one is missing two legs
20. 120 seconds

Math Wizards'
Not Again Georgy!

1. He ran away 12 times
2. 0.5 hours
3. 80 minutes
4. 75 miles
5. 450 feet
6. 0.2 or ⅕ miles per minute
7. 4 miles per hour
8. 18 minutes
9. 2 hours
10. 7.5 miles
11. 4:25 PM
12. 30 minutes
13. 6 minutes
14. He had run away 80 times
15. 15,000 yards
16. 6 hours
17. 50 bees
18. 0.25 miles
19. 12.5 kilometers

Math Wizards'
Can You Imagine Jack Without Jill?

1.	4 times	11.	21 tantrums
2.	6 doors	12.	560 minutes
3.	3 wagons	13.	8 pails of water
4.	120 minutes	14.	6 bottles
5.	5000 milliliters	15.	288 missed calls
6.	3 threats	16.	100 bottles of water received
7.	6 liters of water	17.	4.5 liters of water
8.	5 liters	18.	7.5 hours
9.	96 times	19.	40 times
10.	6 times		

Math Wizards'
Old Innovative MacDonald

1.	4 hours	15.	$2,250
2.	$100	16.	6 hours
3.	7 hours	17.	10,950 visitors
4.	45 minutes	18.	21,900 people
5.	50 gallons	19.	91,250 gallons
6.	$250	20.	$6,125
7.	350 gallons	21.	2,190 hours
8.	210 visitors	22.	1,825 sessions
9.	420 visitors	23.	109,500 people
10.	For 30 days, 1500 gallons. (For 31 days, 1550 gallons.) **	24.	182,500 gallons
11.	$500	25.	$10,075
12.	7 hours	26.	21,900 hours
13.	For 30 days, 1800 people. (For 31 days, 1860 people.)**	27.	109,500 people
14.	18,250 gallons	28.	219,000 people

** Mnemonic Device Reminder: 30 days has September, April, June and November. All the rest have 31 except February, which has 28 days, but in a leap year, which comes once in every four, February then has one day more. - PoetryFoundation.org Leap year poem

Math Wizards'
Mary's Loyal Lil Lamb

1.	20 times	16.	$204
2.	7 days	17.	10.83 days (10 ⅚ days)
3.	4 times	18.	180 times
4.	70 minutes	19.	608 ⅓ hours
5.	4 hours	20.	1,300 days
6.	2 bottles	21.	$820
7.	52 hours	22.	43 ⅓ days
8.	8 times	23.	360 times
9.	3,650 minutes	24.	About 50.7 days
10.	60 days	25.	2,600 days
11.	$90	26.	$1,600
12.	104 hours	27.	2,600 hours
13.	18 times	28.	900 times
14.	60.83 hours (60 ⅚ hours)	29.	3,041 ⅔ hours
15.	520 days	30.	13,000 days

You Did it!

I hope you had a wonderful journey during your time exploring the Budding Young Poets', Math Wizards', and Artists' Zones!

Thank you!

G h